GLOBAL GHOST STORIES

GHOSTS
IN AUSTRALIA

BY PAIGE V. POLINSKY

EPIC

BELLWETHER MEDIA · MINNEAPOLIS, MN

EPIC

EPIC BOOKS are no ordinary books. They burst with intense action, high-speed heroics, and shadows of the unknown. Are you ready for an Epic adventure?

This edition first published in 2022 by Bellwether Media, Inc.

No part of this publication may be reproduced in whole or in part without written permission of the publisher. For information regarding permission, write to Bellwether Media, Inc., Attention: Permissions Department, 6012 Blue Circle Drive, Minnetonka, MN 55343.

Library of Congress Cataloging-in-Publication Data

Names: Polinsky, Paige V., author.
Title: Ghosts in Australia / by Paige V. Polinsky.
Description: Minneapolis, MN : Bellwether Media, 2022. | Series: Epic: global ghost stories |
   Includes bibliographical references and index. | Audience: Ages 7-12 | Audience: Grades 4-6 |
   Summary: "Engaging images accompany information about ghost stories in Australia. The combination
   of high-interest subject matter and light text is intended for students in grades 2 through 7"--Provided
   by publisher.
Identifiers: LCCN 2021011397 (print) | LCCN 2021011398 (ebook) | ISBN 9781644875384 (library binding)
   | ISBN 9781648344466 (ebook)
Subjects: LCSH: Ghosts--Australia--Juvenile literature.
Classification: LCC BF1472.A97 P65 2022 (print) | LCC BF1472.A97 (ebook) | DDC 133.10994--dc23
LC record available at https://lccn.loc.gov/2021011397
LC ebook record available at https://lccn.loc.gov/2021011398

Text copyright © 2022 by Bellwether Media, Inc. EPIC and associated logos are trademarks
and/or registered trademarks of Bellwether Media, Inc.

Editor: Elizabeth Neuenfeldt   Designer: Brittany McIntosh

Printed in the United States of America, North Mankato, MN.

TABLE OF CONTENTS

GHOSTS IN AUSTRALIA   4

MIMI SPIRITS   8

THE MIN MIN LIGHTS   12

FRED THE FRIENDLY GHOST   16

JUST STORIES?   20

GLOSSARY   22

TO LEARN MORE   23

INDEX   24

GHOSTS IN AUSTRALIA

Australia has hundreds of **Indigenous** tribes. Some Indigenous people believe they share the **Outback** with spirits.

DREAMTIME STORIES

Many tribes believe spirits created all living things. Special tales explain how and why. These are called Dreamtime stories.

Some spirits are helpful **ancestors**. Others are monsters. Some stories of spirits are thousands of years old!

British
settler

6

Britain began to **colonize** Australia in 1788. Indigenous people thought **settlers** were ghosts!

Settlers found ghosts of their own. Many were based on Indigenous tales.

MIMI SPIRITS

Tribes in northern Australia believe in Mimi spirits. The spirits taught their ancestors how to paint, hunt, cook, and fish.

Kakadu
National Park
Northern Territory

Ubirr
Rock
Paintings

Nourlangie
Rock
Paintings

Mimi spirit rock painting

Tribes created rock paintings to share the teachings. Today, visitors can see these paintings at Kakadu National Park!

9

SPIRIT PETS

Mimis have all kinds of pets. Some even have pet kangaroos and crocodiles!

Mimi spirits are long and thin. They live inside cracks in rocks.

Mimis only come out at night. They like to hunt and fish in peace. Do Mimis really roam after dark?

THE MIN MIN LIGHTS

Min Min is a **ghost town**. Strange white, yellow, and blue **orbs** float in the air there.

Min Min,
Queensland

ALSO KNOWN AS...

Indigenous people
call the lights
"Dead Men's Campfire."
Another name is
"Debil-Debil."

In some tales, the Min Min lights bob up
and down. In others, they chase people!

Some tribes think the lights are ancestor spirits. They protect the land.

Other tribes believe the lights are evil. They make people disappear! What do you think?

— IS IT TRUE? —

The Min Min lights might be a kind of lightning. They could be a trick of the light. In some cases, they may just be glowing bugs!

FRED THE FRIENDLY GHOST

Theatre Royal is Australia's oldest theater. It is haunted by an actor named Fred. He died in the 1800s. Workers see Fred walking around. Some hear his voice. Late at night, he tells people to leave.

Theatre Royal
Hobart, Tasmania

Once, an actor talked with Fred. She thought he was a stage worker. Then he disappeared!

In 1984, a fire started inside the building. Nobody was there. But the **fire curtain** fell onto the flames. Did Fred stop the fire?

fire curtain

— CULTURAL CONNECTION —

England has its own Theatre Royal in London. Theatre Royal Drury Lane is haunted by a young man in a gray cloak. But actors are happy to see this ghost. Stories say the Man in Gray only appears at successful shows!

JUST STORIES?

Australia is full of ghost stories. Some are thousands of years old.

Are they just stories? Or do ghosts appear in the Outback?

GLOSSARY

ancestors—relatives who lived long ago

colonize—to take control of an area and send people to live there

fire curtain—a heavy curtain that keeps fire from spreading

ghost town—a town that no longer has any people living in it

Indigenous—related to people who have lived in a region from the earliest time

orbs—things that are in the shape of balls

Outback—the part of Australia located far from cities; few people live in the Outback.

settlers—people who move to live in a new region

TO LEARN MORE

AT THE LIBRARY

Ashwin, Kate. *The Night Marcher and Other Oceanian Tales*. Chicago, Ill.: Iron Circus Comics, 2021.

Magrin, Federica. *Atlas of Monsters and Ghosts*. Oakland, Calif.: Lonely Plant Global Limited, 2019.

Polinsky, Paige V. *Ghosts in Europe*. Minneapolis, Minn.: Bellwether Media, 2022.

ON THE WEB

FACTSURFER

Factsurfer.com gives you a safe, fun way to find more information.

1. Go to www.factsurfer.com.

2. Enter "ghosts in Australia" into the search box and click 🔍.

3. Select your book cover to see a list of related content.

INDEX

actor, 16, 18, 19

ancestors, 5, 8, 15

Britain, 6, 7

colonize, 7

Cultural Connection, 19

Dreamtime stories, 5

fire, 19

Fred, 16, 18, 19

ghost town, 12

Indigenous, 4, 7, 13

Is It True?, 15

Kakadu National Park, 8, 9

Man in Gray, 19

maps, 8, 12, 16

Mimi spirits, 8, 9, 10, 11

Min Min, Australia, 12

Min Min lights, 12, 13, 15

name, 13

orbs, 12

Outback, 4, 21

pets, 10

rock paintings, 9

settlers, 6, 7

spirits, 4, 5, 8, 9, 10, 15

Theatre Royal, 16, 19

tribes, 4, 5, 8, 9, 15

The images in this book are reproduced through the courtesy of: PomInOz, front cover (top), p. 20; Claudio Soldi, front cover (bottom), pp. 2-3; Bangkokflame, p. 3; Maurizio De Mattei, pp. 4-5; Lev Kropotov, p. 5; katz, pp. 6-7 (soldier); Regine Poirier, pp. 6-7 (background soldiers); kwest, pp. 6-7 (background); Enrico Della Pietra, pp. 8, 9; Anan Kaewkhammul, p. 10 (kangaroo); John Kasawa, p. 10 (crocodile); Serge Goujon, pp. 10-11, 20-21; World History Archive/ Alamy, p. 11; Ko G.capture, pp. 12-13; oat.s, p. 13; Master1305, p. 14; Elliotte Rusty Harold, p. 15; Hemis/ Alamy, pp. 16-17; Viorel Sima, p. 17; Kamil Macniak, p. 18 (woman); aerogondo2, p. 18 (background); Ferenc Szelepcsenyi, p. 19 (top); Claudio Divizia, p. 19 (bottom); ChameleonsEye, pp. 21, 23.